balloons and stripey trousers

Previous books by Rennie Parker

Secret Villages (Flambard Press, 2001)
Newborough County (Shoestring, 2001)
Borderville (Shoestring, 2011)
Candleshoe (Shoestring, 2014)
The Complete Electric Artisan (Shoestring, 2017)
Jongleur: versions from the troubadours (Shoestring, 2021)

balloons and stripey trousers

RENNIE PARKER

Shoestring Press

All rights reserved. No part of this work covered by the copyright herein may be reproduced or used in any means – graphic, electronic, or mechanical, including copying, recording, taping, or information storage and retrieval systems – without written permission of the publisher.

Printed by imprintdigital
Upton Pyne, Exeter
www.digital.imprint.co.uk

Typesetting and cover design by The Book Typesetters
hello@thebooktypesetters.com
07422 598 168
www.thebooktypesetters.com

Published by Shoestring Press
19 Devonshire Avenue, Beeston, Nottingham, NG9 1BS
(0115) 925 1827
www.shoestringpress.co.uk

First published 2023
© Copyright: Rennie Parker

The moral right of the author has been asserted.

ISBN 978-1-915553-42-3

Acknowledgements

My thanks to *Under the Radar* (issue 22), where 'someday, son, all of this will be yours' first appeared; also 192 online magazine for 'how their nets are entangled', and to the Writing East Midlands Aurora Prize 2022, where 'the desperate life of Monica Jones' was published online.

Most of this collection was written with the help of a work in progress award from the Society of Authors, 2021–22.

Contents

'a warning to the curious'	1
balloons and stripey trousers	2
you will be in this place for a thousand years	3
sent me here for no particular reason	4
no dancing at the Grand Pavilion	7
the habits of successful people	8
speaking & listening, level 1	9
'someday son, all of this will be yours'	11
they will foster resentment in their plastic hearts	13
not in education or employment	15
she says painting calms her down and then does nothing	16
every good boy deserves favour	17
eleven teaching assistants descending a staircase	18
brand new management despair expression	20
real not real	22
hello can i help you	23
I'm on the radio/think they own the planet	24
offering year-round business and enterprise	26
what I had in mind	27
dreadful, these labyrinths	28
not suitable for the post	30
a pause for reflection	32
an erasure poem	34
work mother work mistress work wife	35
the desperate life of Monica Jones	36
positively for one night only	38
poison	40
interlude: anarchy	41
the relative nature of interviews	42
the international collective of artists says no	44
seize the day 'till someone seizes off you	45
and you loved him like a brother	46
the carpet sweepers	47

dreaming about the plenitude   48
how their nets are entangled   49
whatever happened…   50
the rule of three   51
your life in a cardboard box   52
the shipping forecast/exit polls predict   53

'a warning to the curious'

a doorway opens in my head and I think dammit yes,
somewhere a person is describing me as *refreshing*

and where I grew up is remote as Atlantis now, or pre-Reformation
                    Sweden in the age of Gustavus Vasa,

and I'm growing smaller and smaller as your version of me
grows larger: it's *look the district of benefits and no beds,
the wasteland kingdom of straydogs and oilcans*

you wonder why I'm not taking up more space in the world,
even though I ran at the future yelling *yes I am beautiful
                                    and brave*

even while you make me smaller than the papers you write in,
because I don't see your Saturdaynight chipshop bravadoes
                                    and I don't see

your Lawrentian heroes and your cool urban gangsters, your
                    delicious Lucys of the untrodden ways,

because everytime I start/ set foot/ or return I have to disguise
who I am; *and for godsake don't tell them you've got a degree
                    and for godsake don't work in a school...*

somewhere in life there's a journalist telling me all this
about my early years, how aid and parcels still thread their way
                                    along ginnels

and you wonder why I'm not taking up more space in the world
            when too many people have stolen my life already

balloons and stripey trousers

We are all clanging about in the kitchen of half-baked recipes,
                                                                     my friends.

I have plate-glassed my way through it and banged the wrong
                                                                     lid onto the box.

I am at the height for sleeves-in-handles, the drink in my hand
                                                                  flinging backwards

and yes I have trod on the world's rake, fetching the broom-
                                                               stick flat in my face.

I have pedalled to discover no bicycle beneath me, stupidly
loyal because it's not as though I'm the main act or anything
                                                                          no

I'm only the cartoon coyote who is off the cliff

who hasn't realised it yet

you will be in this place for a thousand years

Because the sky has its own nets.
Because the burglar alarms are limpet-mines and other volcanic
                                                            devices.
Because the clock ticks anyway.
Because voices echo from the lead-lined tomb.
Because the Grand Pigeon of the Apocalypse has peered in at
                                                        the window
And he's looking straight at me.
Because the offices lie empty in the grey valley.
Because the street goes straight past us, busy with itself.
Because the other industries here do not exist.
Because the troublesome people come spilling their mania
Because we are the very last option on their list.
Because shadows are moving in the distant rooms beyond the
                                              firedoor of No Approach.
Because the labyrinth will go on until the end of its string.

sent me here for no particular reason

One day all
of this will be gone,
ephemeral jobs.
Flickering light
and the posters, peeling.
Chairs drag back
as if poised for escape.

I must be the nuisance
their leader has warned
them about: whenever
I speak they drop
their files, intent
on worlds of their own.

The false vegetation
blooms with dust;
the catacombs
of all those offices
tower ahead;

it doesn't take much
to bring them back
to a childhood – any
desk will do it,
visual aids. *'Ta-daaa!'*

Symmetrical doors
hide calamitous trash,
games no-one knows,
incomplete sets
the kettle they couldn't
be bothered to fix;

the white banners, old
the wrong name stickered
at the crackly phone,
webcam poised like a gun,

the overcast balconies
rats in a maze,
a PC left there
its chin on the table
and rubble spread out
across somebody's desk.

Three months later
positions don't move.
Stare straight through
I'm not here
(*She's not here*)
heads in the sand... *lalala...*

the same clients round
'*how can we help you*'
the same vague air
like dragged from their orbit
James Bond maybe,
deep cover ops

...*mayday mayday...*
...*left with these people...*
over and out
too bad, too late
you should have said.
Six months later
one of them cracks:
previous job.

All I can do
is wave them goodbye
as buses grind past
on the dual-use plaza
its fountains switched off
and the bank which bears
the city's proud name.

You won't like it
(and they were right)
the feet, bags trailing
the rooms beyond doors,

half an hour
just half an hour left
until we detach,
the module returning
to thud in the desert
a lifetime away.

no dancing at the Grand Pavilion

The silent houses are holding their breath,
second cars parked like hearses at the rear
dark sandstone, blocky, with the shutters down:

empty except for the tree-cutter's roar
as he prepares for another out-of-town buyer
for another sub-baronial seafront pile –

but the tide's gone out: and homecoming cars
squash between narrow entries not built for them
with tired commuters from other people's towns,

while daisies bloom in the cracked flags
of a once-promoted tourist view
all restoration paused.

the habits of successful people

You are there, lunging at the phone before
anyone else can get it – always in first, the laptop open
earlier and earlier,

you batter the keyboard searching for an answer
and why are you there at five o'clock and beyond
still driving, being driven,
are you looking for your moment in the sun?

What will happen to you, serf,
when they are bored with your home life
and your mild infirmities?

Hands up for the next task
the scraps from our managers, hanging
onto every word from the screech-owl senior leader,

twenty more years at the same desk
lording it over your rivals at the annual review,
the tickbox of your little existence
present and correct:

how often I feed your ego
treading on eggshells cast
by your brittle empire,

> your expectations are high/low/not achieved;
> your target is x
> your lucky colour is greige,
> your saint is St. Perpetua of the Twelve Immaculate Ways.

speaking & listening, level 1

Four months later they are still not talking.
Memories of the banking sector:
girls doing paperwork, all they are fit for.
I'm just not organised he says
with that calculated laugh.

The cluttered office topples with files.
Pots pile, the great unwashed.
Other staff bend their backs,
heads toward screens.

Stranger things have happened –
flowers on a windowsill –
but now they have taken their flowers away
we must all begin again.

He blooms red, looks finished.
'Stay off the booze,' I tell him:
there's always more where you came from
thinking whenever you blag your way
some girl will be convinced.

Mr. Talent, he brims:
I'm a glass half full kinda guy
always on the offchance –
the students believe in him
but the careworn staff, they don't.

Expect he stays: so real, disarming
gladhanding the populace
like a smalltown elected mayor
even though he flunked the lot

missed his deadlines, forgot his gear,
lost plans, exams, the evidence.
His class will have to sit their test a second time
happy, even grateful, in the dark.

'someday son, all of this will be yours'

The walls are tacked with sockets like
the world's technology is here
behind a Salvation Army shop
and its vacant commercial partners.

Boards give positive feedback
all worthy bright assertions
declaiming modest ambitions
in the wake of benefit sanctions –

alarms are clipped onto walls
the empty flower-trough yawns,
I wait for something to happen
but the staff will not be pressed:

their hostile secretary glares
as though I'm the one who's failed
and high above our heads
an ancient heater rattles.

It's not about what you can do
it's not about what you've done
each one of the claimants knows
it's whether you fit the plan –

they'll keep you marking time
as long as their salaries slot in
for jobs that don't exist, can't be got
can't be made to happen

each one of the claimants knows
however much you can do

you're over the line mate, and
your chances are shot –

it's thirty hours a week
to prove you're still in the game
while a chuntering copier pours
the endless patter of forms.

Our manager outlines a tree
I help them stick up the leaves
they write their messages on:
it helps when I believe…

I thank you for your time…
I know I can achieve…
opposite empty units where
the businesses have gone.

they will foster resentment in their plastic hearts

How did they get like this, your friends
who smiled on the very first day,

the fear and the sweat and the fine mist
adrenalin and brightly-coloured games –

like teenagers under a halogen light
in the butcher's shop of the world.

Look they will say and *look, look
at the hot new work I am accomplishing*,

they will shriek and whoop like macaws
at the end-of-season meeting.

Alas! Flare! Alas! Flare!
you might signal your discontent

and your face is up at the window
like a trapped Victorian apprentice, but

one of them will be there in a polyester dress
grinning as you go down,

they have run through the repertoire
of the photographs on their faces,

the smears and lipstick and the red-meat taint
one eye fixed on the air above your head –

ah they let you fall in, the chasm widens
at each misdemeanour,

'what was that you said?' they snap
as their personal doors slam shut –

and how did they get like this, your *friends*
who smiled on the very first day,

as they hustle closer together
like covered wagons in the American West

corralled against wolves, against you,
they are walking reversed from the sight of you,

having the whole table to themselves.

not in education or employment

Smalltown badboy girlmagnet hey
even though you cannot remember your own passwords
you swagger on down the suburban road
like Mr. John Wayne on the streets of Laredo.

What will happen when the pills wear off
Mr. Charisma, spinning the waltzers,
one day soon the voices in your head
will tell you what they mean,
and the girls on your internet fix
think you're The One.

What will happen when the pills wear off,
hardly able to string one word:
you are going to be the man-child
who drives the teachers crazy
and they won't let you go,

Mr Green Man in your surly everglade
choosing from all the flowers on the internet
and none of them will know.

she says painting calms her down and then does nothing

You bounce off the walls of your own condition
infecting yourself with trouble
as though the world's got your number;
and today you can't be pinned down
as the mercury rises in your veins
it's the high-wire act as the staff
attempt to talk you around,
and your classmates think it's the circus
and they only say they love you because
they want you displayed in front of them
like a choice anatomists' doll, its heart:

you fix it together like this
and you fix it together like that, ricochet
from one dazed ghost-train to another
swerving the yes/no interface as ideas
fly past your head at the speed of light.

every good boy deserves favour

They pay for me – extras, talks, people who know,
decisions in rooms, closed doors.
Once, a person talked with me for a full hour
small eyed, persuasive; but no.

The needs of a monarch
an absolute one,
my face on the coinage and primetime TV –
they maraud my idyll with its cameras
these local clotpolls
with their half-formed ideas,
fit only for turnips.

Unnatural parents have brought me to this:
I wear my saintly hoodie
as far over my head as it will go,
my voice the reckoning.

Papers… I cut a swathe.
Send them to the four corners of the empire.
Listen to me, my people –
there, the Sun King has spoken.
I have kicked out your lights
and set you in opposition.

It is time for my afternoon rest
on the pockmarked desk in 15A –
humble, a dun classmate
attending at my elbow with a proffered cola-can,

the dizziness of my fall
an astonishment, even now.

eleven teaching assistants descending a staircase

Even though such a thing would be useless in a real emergency
our instructor unfolds the chair.

Now pulled into position like a dentists' throne
we're ready to hurtle on down the track.

I observe the crooked pinball machine
that is Stairway 8A, second floor.

I hurt myself today goes the song
from an adolescent wi-fi

as Laura bumps down one step at a time
its runners grazing cross-ply over the treads

to see if she can feel.
'Not too fast!' she calls

as the blunt equipment capitulates,
Becky gripping the handrail like

she's mowing the lawn or polishing,
steering this floating spectacle

that is our sharp-angled descent.
Our students are in their safe classroom beyond

as we do the danger for them,
we adults plunging down a stairwell –

and they too are dragging themselves
exams, exams, painfully

under the swishing fan and the slanted rays.
You can have it all… the song explains

but not quite yet:
there's Jacob who can't read

and Chloe, whose main aim is
to haul herself through each day.

They already have their empire of dirt,
no song is assigned to help them

but the staff are – each one of us
redundant, redirected, redeployed

the bruised images of our former selves
on dusty ledges at home,

our *what have I become*
still ringing in our ears

as we scrape the chair back up
like miners with an empty bucket,

the stairwell is our shaft
where the bright cage descends.

brand new management despair expression

> *'normally, normally/As if already mad'*
> ('The Halls of Bedlam', Robert Graves)

He was recognised at work
the boss knew him personally
golf on Fridays
the loan of his caravan,
a responsible man.

He ruled the lines
he picked up his briefcase
day at the office
just as expected,
each must suffice.

And fault lines appear
when continents slide
sideways, down
internal riot rife
a sense not his own

as the hand of wildness
grasps the slow heart,
the quiet ones break first
easily, meekly
because they are ready.

A fine day in autumn
when beech masts beat the roof
of his executive saloon –
a modest nature
that never caused harm…

The neighbours turn out
they didn't expect it
though fearful at noises
in wheel-clamped suburbia
jumping at shadows,

then scatter indoors
pretending as always
that nothing will happen
that nothing is so
that people are happy

people like them
the responsible ones
with children, and wives.
Their front doors stay shut
another day, another dollar

for sweet-talking friends
in inverted commas,
dinner-party fixtures,
chatty acquaintances,
job-stealing twitchers,

new-model citizens
polished desirables
too good to live with
a house up for sale
in '*such a nice district*'.

They still don't believe it
back at the office
the brand new replacement,
the waters closed over,
the clock on the mantelpiece
ticking, and ticking.

real not real

so the stiff-haired personnel have managed you into submission
and it's been years now.
I watch you in the guise of a Woman Who Knows.
Time was – and is – a traitor
pulling back from everyone
who put their trust in Her
and the adverts with their seductive ways
their effortless talk of dynamo start-up industries
on various purpose-built estates:
how vigorous and intent
the faces of their brave young men! how taut
the stretched skins with their fuelled enmities,
and you islanded, a pariah
the broken bridge attempting to ford a river
while the foul tide swivels past –
those choice roles awarded
to one who *fits the needs of today's environment*
when what they mean is 'young',
hating yourself and what they will become
unable to leave the race,
they are pinning their rivals to the dartboard
with their casual cruelties
and you, rejected for no reason
facing the same people again and again
every session a marketplace
every market a butcher's hall;
it's you they've got on the slab.

hello can i help you

i'm a peopleperson me and that's what they told me at the clinic and i couldn't believe it when they made me a supervisor here:

so put the sign on OPEN kelley because we don't want them to think we are shut now do we –

– if our visitor figures plummet it's your job on the line kelley not mine because i'm a full timer that's why

[it doesn't do to have them getting above themselves now does it]

WHO FOLDED THESE TEATOWELS THE LABELS SHOULD BE ON THE *TOP*

i'll be checking in future kelley there's nothing like a little mysteryshopper exercise to keep you on your toes

it's a stressful job you know very stressful this very but i don't suffer from stress not really not any more no not after the counselling

because i'm a peopleperson me and i'm here to serve the public and let's face it tourism is the world and the world is tourism

[beam] *hellocanihelpyou?*

I'm on the radio/think they own the planet

these people, right, they see our town on the telly and they
                           want to retire here, don't they.
That's all it takes, just some costume bash and they're phoning
                           that office like lemmings.

And they think it's gonna to be like that, like what they've seen
                           on the box… they see us *once*,
that's all it takes. Believe me, you wanna convert your old guest
                           house to a goldmine

get on the box. Any way you can. Me, I went down the seafront
                           when they were filming
24 hours a day: it were mad, some guy on a wind-machine
                           and a lass throwing leaves…

Not that I'm saying our guesthouses are bad but some of them are
                           Oi you
quite nice once you get past the plywood and swirlypattern nylon
                           rugs – I mean OK

you have to give credit, credit where it's due, they really try hard
                           these folks round here
but I've been in building you see, and I know. Tourism you see,
                           tourism is this country's

cash-cow innit, and half of us wouldn't be here if it weren't for
                           them coachloads. **Oi**
I mean none of us would actually choose to run this type of
                           establishment, would they?

You wouldn't say to your teachers at school hey when I grow up
                           I wanna run like: a SHOP
on Esplanade Drive. They'd say get a life & what about qualifi-

cations and that? well I've got

qualifications and that so I'm tellin you straight... these people
they don't give a toss
'cos all they want is what everyone's got, but without them having
to work for it or pay

and then they retire to places like this, and for once in my
lifetime I'm winning.
Not that I'm saying there's anything wrong but I'd soon be out
of a job 'cos they're bas/

unpleasant, some of these people; clicking their fingers like
you're some kind of waiter
rapping their knuckles on the counter when they think you
can't see 'em, jabbing their

fingers in your face and counting the pennies back out v e r y
s l o w l y and fumbling
as if you've given the wrong change and – **Oi, what does it
take to get served round here**

I once went down to the Grand Hotel at 2 a.m. and stuck my 4
mill chisel in all their tyres.
Me and my mate we once climbed up a signpost, right, and we
turned the signs round.

Headlines two weeks running, *Target & Leader*. That'll teach
'em I say, this tourist nation:
nobody ever found out. But I was born round here and we hate
'em moving in with their

money and four-by-fours. **Oi you, are you serving here
or what?** Just keep your wig on
can't you see this girl's got a microphone? okay sunshine
now what do you want

offering year-round business and enterprise

Discovering a long-abandoned shop with its newspapers
                                        yellowing in foetid air
I see it is not yet dead: because shuffling forward on a damp
                                                cardboard mat
comes the owner, crepuscular, blinking and hesitant, bemused
                                        at seeing a customer.

I point at the handwritten sign on the counter where squashed-
                                        up descended letters
in faded marker say: *Sandwiches. Egg. Salmon and Cucumber.*
                                                Tinned Sardine
and Fresh Tomato. I ask for the Salmon and Cucumber. Ten
                                        minutes later I emerge

with Sardine & Fresh Tomato stuffed in a squarebox designed
                                        for a baked potato.
The hanging overhead sign squeaks grimly like an old forced
                                                gate as I pass
like a wraith into what should be drifting sepulchral sea-mist
                                        from Wrangle Ness.

Their lids were torn, sticking up, hanging off, one box piled on
                                        another and then
collapsed inside itself – on shallow ledges behind the till there
                                                were screwtop
containers with kola kubes and orange balls, sherbert lemons
                                        and midget gems.

what I had in mind

meanwhile it is clear from my researches that we'll never attract a better class of person unless we invest in *facilities*.

and when the New Albert Watmough Centenary Memorial Jubilee Hall stands proudly on this exact spot my vision will have been vindicated.

because you cannot expect rich americans to sit on little orange plastic chairs.

and it's not even signposted.

at the very least we should get rid of those net curtains.

and replace the lean-to shed with a first floor mezzanine.

we are living in a service economy I might add and we have to capitalise on our *natural assets*.

and during my inaugural year I aim to bring about a total renaissance of our local business economy

through a natural re-focus on what it is our great little town does best.

and just the other day when I was taking my grand-daughter along to her forest school mathematics and tumbletots outreach genius workshop

I realised what it was. cream teas.

dreadful, these labyrinths

Falling as a particle through space he remembers that he should
                              have prepared for this.
You are no comet, no shooting star:
a pinhead of angels, dancing.

The shock of it pulls him up
a parachutist, attached by the feet –
and where – what – the hanged man.
His arms windmill, yes, because he (believe it or not)
                     a broken thread
               he,
he should have prepared.

The outpour! so many sentences from the glib
the eloquent, the look-at-me-observing-myself, a *being*
being *is*

and how he is acting the part of it
the ineffable celeb – yes – in flight, caught
in a crossfire of headlights now:
no anecdote can save him,
no how poor how disadvantaged my past.

Like the whale plummeting on through the wrong universe in
                                     the comedy
at some point there will be contact
(it may or may not be pleasant)
– and the air has gone off-kilter
like a bad smell, the knowledge that something has moved
                            is moving/will have moved

the abstract God of Panic watching him back and look
he (or He) is surprised –

another unique facet,

let's have it out there displayed,

the trick is: to keep balancing

on that pinhead

not suitable for the post

Let's have a conversation about it, let's pretend this is not
a jobshare or one without a desk or a laptop or even a room
to sit in: you like to think you're different every time, so let's
imagine we are those mavericks and avatars who ride
 the sole purpose of our light.

Tell me you're not that public convenience converted into
a 'multi-purpose arts hub', let us consider, all other things
being equal, whether this job is genuine as in not immediately
scheduled for oblivion like your empty venues when
 the money goes astray –

maybe you spent the whole year's budget on novelty spoons
and contracts for your mates, where the girlfriend or
the daughter of the chairman will get it, where you ask me
how long I've waited or when I'll be moving on, because
 it's not like I'm ever wanted – maybe I'm

destined for that low-fi existence our energy-savers delight in;
so thank you for your time, it's as bad as keeping a score-
sheet under the desk where you're playing Candidate Bingo
again, or coming clean, explaining that what you really wanted
 was a man, or someone

older/younger, less or more experienced or in fact anyone
except the person in front of you now… and thank you for
your attitude, *we'll knock that nonsense out of you* implied
by each aggressive jobsworth as I'm ushered towards
 the Department of Last Chance Saloons…

No, it's not like the one where an assistant screamed
that she loved her boss right there (no comment) not forgetting
the one who wore pyjamas and said: *I don't normally dress like
this at interviews*; or the one who said: *we're not supposed
                                    to be in this room today*

and: *sorry we can't refund your expenses now.*

a pause for reflection

disguising my age… *Jeezus*… and the familytalk and the
                              stereotypes

it's a long-haul trek across the horizon.

Maybe it was always my fault.

Maybe I should have been s e x y (note to self) maybe it was
the career-enhancing voluntary work I didn't do
as the temps were made into permanents,

maybe it was the green shoes or the red dress? Maybe
I was being so 'useful' they loved me in the backroom,
a short-term contract only?

Trust me, I cannot see above the applications now. I apply and
                                                       apply
I sell and sell

I need a platform, a ladder, a someone-doing-the-rounds-on-
                                             my-behalf,
an eye for the main chance; worse

I need a pocketful of steely smiles,
the kind of sincerity that's believed in.

For I am paper-thin these days, with masks aplenty.
I can show and turn with the best of them.
Show and turn.

Maybe the dirigible of my hopes and dreams

is bumping along the grass

like a half-inflated rugby ball, maybe

I should have been anything other than a single unattached female in want of a job.

an erasure poem

Key to success: mentors who 'talented' one who *mattered*, blah

Little did I know I was the wrong sort of person from the start

and *their* parents' incomes, allthewayback to the days of
                                        Methuselah or so it felt –
somehow not oh like the swishyhaired ones with their own
                                       bijou wardrobes, and
no amount of certificates could turn
this sow's ear into a fluting silver reed;
uncomfortable in meetings and side-eyed by the Henriettas
                 and Sophies with their artsy flippant ways

– meanwhile, what are they wanting in this fractured world?
                                                             I had
the kind of bathroom you would find in a condemned property
                 which even a Dickensian orphan would avoid

besides: *'if you're so clever, why aren't you rich'* the refrain,
the refrain   why don't you (for instance)   the refrain, plus:
                                      'if you snooze you lose'

what was I thinking back then? sign up, sign up
there's ones who will name their price   never occurred
that my likelihood of landing a dreamjob was
                                                             remote as
flying to Venus   with the aid of a party-balloon

work mother work mistress work wife

Everything a problem you find yourself in. What did those
                              oldwives warn you about back then?
No safety net… *get married and go away…*

of course it wouldn't last: spare female, no *cachet*. What have I
                                done to deserve this.

The audience, in the audience as the notable men stride past.
Every dullard a genius in their eyes, climbing onto the platform
                        with a file of useful contacts –

lost count of the times.
We thought you'd like this little corner over here, we thought you
                                    wouldn't mind…

and their serving-women would have you stacking chairs at the
main event, stacking chairs and buttering scones like them *('it's*
                                          only me')

there's always room for one more, on the cutprice conveyor-
belt: *we need an extra hand in here/these goods won't sell themselves*

and the work-wives stand at the threshold with: I could have
                                    told you this,
they'll walk straight past you, eyes fixed, aren't you insulted yet?

the desperate life of Monica Jones

You cannot imagine what it takes
to get inside any charmed circle
beached in the English Midlands, the one
aquamarine in a whole desert of pebbles.
Each year our faces peer back at us
from holiday snaps, the very same spectacles
the same shrewd levelling gaze – and he
he says he wants me serious
while he fantasises the girls he cannot have:
younger, less aware.
If anyone asks me what I did with my wonderful life
I will say I was an actress, because
you cannot be the midwife unto genius
while being an actual wife, you know;
I amuse him with curt pleasantries
at this or that new function, like the queen
who is destined for oblivion after nine days.
Two others I hear of –
the common drabs, I call them
I'd have their eyes on a platter if I could
their movements kill me –
my audience while I front it out
plated to his side like the Incredible Twin
wielding my magnificence abroad
a headscarf the ensign
like those Hull women he professes to despise
in his deathless verse.
Fated, I tell you,
like one of those Classical vixens
the Furies always clattering at my back
the populace drinking the lies
put about by Palace attendants
as I choose not their games, which I am good at,

but him alone, the show
forcing me off my own stage
and I know how they hate me,
the office girls with their witless prattle
disturbing my wasted hours
while *he* says I must endure
endure for him of course, and not for myself.
Yes, I am the woman he would have been –
the wasp in the trap,
look at our landscapes here, all rocks,
journeying infinite barrenness
to the utter collapse of stars.

positively for one night only

Novelty my friend is not in short supply
just as the weather
and people's minds are turned:
a silver swan, the Famous Two-Headed Calf,
notions and hints.
I used to share a platform with the Master himself
known across four continents:
now anyone can do it
they need not stir outside on a night like this.

    I set out my table at the Mechanics' Institute
    room for less than a hundred seated
    – they'll not miss a thing, blast 'em –
    bare boards, a chiming clock
    packed crinolines on three seats,
    hush of the flaring gas
    all eyes on me.

'Your cabinets will not hold, bolted together like that' she shrills
                  – a new girl, untried –
Listen, there is so much misdirection in the average home
with its player-pianos and folderols
that no-one never need visit a travelling magic show again.
We are both reduced, my friend –
equipment in storage
carpet-bagging to the next insalubrious hotel
relying on sleight-of-hand to realise our bread.

I have done myself out of a job, Ermintrude
and you need not stay for the encore
there now –
don't cry –

on with the greasepaint girl the audience will be here
expecting a Henry Irving
not Bevis Croucher who left ten years before
his life in a pressed-cardboard suitcase
with no reputation to speak of.

poison

'I had to get rid of her, sitting there so dull and plain.
She fills up envelopes for us, occasionally
A volunteer,
Nobody really.
She'd never have changed the subject.
God, I have to get back in time for two.

Are you here long yourself? I hate it
When people attract your attention, isn't it weird,
I have to be very nasty. *Very* nasty.

She's a little disconnected, that is all –
I'm used to her
But now she's gone we can truly communicate
And if you're still suffering from
That terrible fish we had,
I have the rescue remedy right here. Not

The real one, you understand,
But this one's just the same. Six drops
Are all it takes…'

interlude: anarchy

Is it a snake, he said.

Silence.

Does that look like a snake to you? he said,
pointing at a picture of a horse.

Of course it's not a snake. Why is that man
pointing at a picture of a horse?

No answer.

What else do your snakes look like?
Is that a giraffe?

If you say so.

All right class -
hands up those who know how to write their names.

Good.

We know where to start from.

the relative nature of interviews

Jets go searching the valley at ripcord speed.
I'm here for a job I don't want and can't get.

Commerce and diggers heap yellow spoil,
the caged workmen roar –

a speculator builds his brand new hotel
on the site of a demolished old hotel

in a village composed entirely of other hotels.
I'm here watching this from a deserted cafe

where a gaunt assistant pushes a lank mop.
I'll call it 'Heartbreak Hotel'

as the mournful English tourists are banking their cars
from here to slatey Ambleside in its cave of rain.

It is a sewer of a road, the only road there is
this is the road I am on, the pressure-pipe

and my interview goes like a slow expected accident
where all the dashboard lights appear

and you know you must stop the car.
At Kendal the lights will say Green:

beyond us only space and the liquid empire,
our great blue signboards with Home written large:

what were you doing with your joke job going for another joke
                                                interview

    they ask,

and I tell the monumental signs as they swipe away
I was on the Alternative Route

where I say: *I will give it careful consideration*
meaning: *this is a terrible mistake*

where I am sitting with my head in my hands *oh no oh no oh no*
at the junction of a road or two rivers

as in the best dilemma scenes
having failed the great connection.

I am so not right for this job
I will push myself through it regardless

I will come all this way at any time, knowing
I should have stayed where I was.

the international collective of artists says no

The twilight years had never looked so good
from the leather-backed deep corner office
the approving senior manager
who loved your way with a press release.
Now you fancy yourself as a connoisseur of the arts
and your brains are departing along with your hair
after a lifetime of sub-committees and cheap PA's,
your orations the word of God
at the firm's annual conference
in the slab-built venue off the interchange.
Little corporate man the game is truly over;
it is unlikely given your age and range of experience,
the results of our psychometric test. We say that art
is not the next pre-retirement seminar
taught in a windowless cubicle
on the downward commute to the grave.
It is far too late I am telling you:
the transport of choice has left that particular station
be content with your bungalow in the suburbs
which artists do not usually have – and the pension,
yes, the pension, which artists do not usually get.
Return to your sunset desk at the landfill job
take up gardening for instance or billiards
go sit in the park with the rest of the deadbeats
a can of flat Special at your knee – because
who will listen to your reasons
after the latest departmental sackings
you who'd never thought about art until now?
The International Collective of Artists says No
their rejection is in the post
along with your P45.

seize the day 'till someone seizes off you

Let's say it wasn't you: what would you say?

The slack-jawed aliens treat her like toxic goods
they think, tapping the table,
what does it take to push her over the edge.

They are talking to each other
like people erasing her carefully
with everyday rubbers and signs,

her reference books are not where they were,
her keys have gone, and soon
her chair will be removed,

she is down the hall on a folded coat
the exit is clear, and yet
she is up and down their staircase, asking

what do they want from her next?
They are shaking their heads
because nothing is right; it seems

everyone else is waiting for her to fall,
there are words in the staffroom: *what
is she doing, still here,*

part of the furniture now
they congratulate themselves
on who they have selected;

here comes the time they will lock the doors.

and you loved him like a brother

Even Muriel thinks you're a fool
one born every minute she says, emptying the shredder
and while you need him for his deft

approval of your crashing plans –
he's there, poised, leaning in
praising your fruitless attempt to beat back the critics.

Wherever he gets his details we can't tell
and now he's reeling you in, poor sucker
saying he knows, he knows.

He's marking the days off the week
asking questions; he's around
me like a fly, eyebrows raised

noting things down on charts which he never shows.
An arms' length away, shielding his calls
always present at the meetings

where he nods and gives the word.
Taking advantage when someone isn't here,
crossing their names off the list.

the carpet sweepers

Go early, come back late –
the balding guy has switched his attention
to one who finds him impressive;
bored officials lob
their comments across the chipboard wall
like tennis in slow motion.
All day long he walks up and down
the festering loop-pile carpet –
he likes to think we think we know he's busy,
this is the time he buys with his degrees.
His volunteers will not come in
it's down to me, I'm punching
the endless data in
and grants are riding on the outcome:
money's there for nothing
you know the way they feel it
by their brief dismissive smiles.
A heavyset person jangles past
swinging on the keys
of her own little kingdom –
look, they have it made
they cannot be removed,
they have their special bunker
with its entry-phones and styles,
a barricade of cabinets
they might be found behind.
Their job descriptions tell us how
they were important once: and now
they bat the hesitant callers away
as though customers are flies.

dreaming about the plenitude

a lifetime of holidays is killing them perfect
with the beautiful children, their artless arrangement:
their mothers, honed down like bone flutes,
that strain – or there, poised quite
like rare *ikebana* in the classical style
with five types of olives
or delicate at the piano perhaps or stuffing
pimientoes with hand-reared lemongrass straight
from a double-page spread about interiors
or careless with artisan bread,
the rich delivery promised: a husband
ironic with stubble and rough linen
cool at his infinite desk, the blond wood and the textiles.

You know they're only pretending but it's so good
at the grandstand window in a hipster cafe
or crunching across wet pebbles as if in the moment
windswept thinking of lighthouses
yanking their dogs back and striding, the world mastered,
a flint-stuck cottage where everything happens
each startled blue summer, those indigo nightfalls
of laughter-echoing parties
the trug encrusted with warm earth
a descending line of wellingtons
in their honey-dappled hallway, matted
with sea-grass and on-point architectural salvage

how their nets are entangled

on the tidal drift in smalltown occupations
why their staff keep leaving and coming back again
reluctant old retainers who are never quite gone:

you would think they had been in these places forever
the only ties they have known, too tight
to let go of, even though they are sinking, sinking

like one of those houses in a remote field
the tenant farmers having absented themselves
long ivy pulling at the crusted stone,

still nameless when their desks are cleared.
And you think the horizon must be bouncing them back
ensuring whoever is born here can't escape

because there is nowhere else but here
the pull of this room, these chairs
the cardigans hanging carelessly across them

whether it is five minutes or ten years.

whatever happened…

Whatever happened to the likely lad?
you're into the furnace once again
and the safer bet who wasn't employed
is taking a chance in a different one-horse town.
Maybe he's having the problems you would have had.

They will spite and charge at the head of department now,
a dunderheaded rhino, all blunt
hitting the fence – he'll say it's not his fault
the other department wanted it like this
his hands are tied, he'll say

and they're staring you back like a row of tinned fish
aghast that you are there, that you exist
while the safer bet who wasn't employed
is taking a chance in a different one-horse town.

the rule of three

...and I walk through the door thinking *this time it's going to work/this time it's going to work/this time it's going to work...*

It was the last time and the time before. Dinosaur time.

OK let's go! and you know this is why we have so many Ofsteds, why so many people have left, why so many others are married to those who are already here – the game

is DEFINITELY ON, I'll capitalise
on the general level of competence here,

the files come out from the bin marked delete,
I could have been a contender, me,
if they don't know how to run applications or who on earth has applied and what on earth it was for

there's a pretty good chance I'll succeed.

your life in a cardboard box

You're on your own and no mistake: the office party is the same
                                           nightmare
look, the lit stages are pulsing with hot flesh

the usual suspects are at the quiche, your line-manager
                                       dispensing warm fizz
as we are told about the targets of our lives.

Now the team-leaders are shiny-bright and wrecked at the talk
                                           of new redundancies;
it feels as though a part of them has died

(*'so many years for this'*)

How long will the payoffs last with prices the way they are?
                                   already the plastic champagne-
flutes are on the floor

the balloon's gone up, bumping the rafters – consultations will
                                              start tomorrow,
until then my friends, enjoy

your tiny betrayals were worth it

cake is served in the lobby as lights go out across the complex,
exit down the back stairs while the office plants are being binned

the shipping forecast/exit polls predict

…low… Fastnet… losing its identity
Humber, Thames, Dover, rain for a time at first
Redcar, Sedgfield, Bishop Auckland
moderate to central good, occasionally poor
upright listening to the forecast
Cromarty, Forth and Tyne, becoming cyclonic
backing north-west Workington
severe gale nine and falling, imminent
Bassetlaw and Bolsover
the land sliding underneath them
hands raised at the guttering lanterns
Don Valley, Rother Valley
lost like their steam-driven industries
swimming further asunder and drowning helpless,
a red wall breached across the midlands
and here it comes the outcrash,
Cape Wrath seas in fury
rivers of wrecks and everything held dear
small furniture and houses the upset tables, hands raised
as results flood into living-rooms
the turbulence running past them:
North Utsire and South Utsire
boulders shouldered aside and upturned trolleys
Trafalgar, Fitzroy, Sole, decreasing slowly
new wolves baying on the foreshores
Dogger, Fisher, German Bight
warning of gales in all areas,
and while you cling to your rock
as the seas rage limitless around you
pray for the ones who most needed this night
as the red castles fell, you shades among shades
a trawler riding asleep on its dark blue ocean
nets cut drifting past Forties and South East Iceland